Sea Eagles

naturally scottish

SCOTTISH NATURAL HERITAGE

© Scottish Natural Heritage 2006
ISBN 1 85397 461 7 paperback
A CIP record is held at the British Library
IA2K0506

Acknowledgements:

Author: John Love (SNH)

Series Editor: Lynne Farrell (SNH)

Design and production: SNH Publishing Unit

Photographs: nialbenvie.com 5, 11, 18, 26; **Pete Cairns** frontispiece, 2, 6 bottom, 27, 28; **Laurie Campbell** opposite contents, opposite introduction, 20; **Laurie Campbell/SNH** 6 (left), 7 (bottom); **Mark Hamblin** front cover, back cover, 8, 9, 25; **Miguel Lasa** 29; **John Love** 22 (both), 23 (both), 24; **P & A Macdonald/SNH** 12; **Neil McIntyre** 19; **Richard Welsby** 15.

Illustrations: Keith Brockie 3, 10, 17; **John Love** 4; **Claire Hewitt** 7 top.

Map: Wendy Price 13.

Scottish Natural Heritage
SNH Publishing Unit
Battleby
Redgorton
Perth PH1 3EW
Tel: 01738 458530
Fax: 01738 458613
E-mail: pubs@snh.gov.uk
www.snh.org.uk

Cover photograph:
Adult sea eagle in flight

Frontispiece:
Adult sea eagle feather detail

Back cover photograph:
Adult sea eagle with fish

Sea Eagles

naturally scottish

by

John Love

(Scottish Natural Heritage)

Foreword

If we adapt George Orwell's maxim to state that whilst 'all birds are equal, some are more equal than others' it still rings true and there is no finer example than the Sea eagle. Many of our raptors are feted for their beauty, shape and form and also for their agility and speed. But if there is one quality which this species truly exhibits it is simply...presence. Like many others I still find it impossible to turn my binoculars onto a Sea eagle without drawing a breath and saying 'Wow'. Even distant views of these great rectangular 'flying doors' cannot fail to evoke awe.

As you will read in this booklet, people did a great deal of harm to this species, through misdeed, mischief and mistake and terminated its tenure on the craggy coast of the British Isles. Some 60 years later, after a change of conscience, and through a ground-breaking project, conservationists have successfully re-introduced this totemic animal. I remember looking at grainy black and white photographs of scruffy eaglets perched on their 'kennels' in the 1970s and feeling so distant from this bird. But as a teenager in the south of England researching the humble kestrel for a school project, it wasn't just the geography that separated us. It was also the improbability of the scheme's success in the face of apathy, persecution and egg-collecting and the clear difficulties which faced the small team of pioneers. I never dared dream that one day I'd have the privilege to stand in cold, driving rain on a wintery Hebridean coast and watch one of these birds strafe by. Then ten years later, I visited a hide to watch live CCTV pictures of young eaglets picking at their food, snapping at flies and soaring down onto the clear Scottish air as they exercised their wings. Fantastic! How refreshing to be able to enjoy and champion this great success in an age when it is all too easy to focus on doom and forthcoming gloom. The dedicated crew who made it happen, to whom we are all indebted, have proved that if you reach for the stars you can earn your eagles and make a real difference.

Being Sea eagles, their habits and ecology mean they are still not that accessible. To get really cracking views, you still have to work hard on the hills, in the glens and along the shores. At least we can all now dream of one day being in the right place at the right time to peer for a moment into that sunlit eye.

Chris Packham
Naturalist and Broadcaster

The distinctively 'fingered' wing-tips and the white tail are characteristic of the adult sea eagle *Haliaeetus albicilla*

Contents

Clàr Innse

Iolaire sùil na grèine - the eagle with the sunlit eye

Introduction Ro-ràdh

The eagle with the sunlit eye Iolaire sùil na grèine

Sea or fish eagles are a group of eight species belonging to the genus *Haliaeetus*. They are more closely related to vultures and kites than to 'true' eagles, such as the familiar golden eagle. The sea eagle *Haliaeetus albicilla* occurs across Asia, Scandinavia, Iceland and part of Greenland. It once occurred throughout Britain.

> 'The white-tailed eagle usually chooses for its retreat some lofty precipice overhanging the sea, and there in fancied security forms its nest and reposes at night.'

William Macgillivray, Descriptions of the Rapacious Birds of Great Britain, 1886.

When William Macgillivray was a boy in Harris, the white-tailed or sea eagle was quite a common sight in the Hebrides. Indeed the Gaelic language has several names for this well-known bird of prey – *Iolaire mhara* translates literally as 'sea eagle', and *Iolaire chladach* as 'shore eagle' while Gaelic even distinguishes the darker, more mottled juvenile as *Iolaire bhreac* or *riabhach*. But the most lyrical of all is surely the poetic term *Iolaire sùil na grèine* – 'the eagle with the sunlit eye'.

Sadly, by the time Macgillivray became Professor of Natural History at Aberdeen University and wrote a book about British birds of prey, the sea eagle was a rare sight indeed. Robert Gray, a famous naturalist at the time, had already reported in his Birds of the West of Scotland (1871) that:

> 'It is impossible to conceal the fact that if the present destruction of eagles continues we shall soon have to reckon this species amongst the extinct families of our 'feathered nobility'.'

The species last bred in Britain in 1916 and became extinct two years later. One of the last nests in Scotland was on the Isle of Rum in 1909 and it is appropriate that this island in the Inner Hebrides, a National Nature Reserve (NNR), should serve as a springboard for a brave reintroduction programme run jointly by Scottish Natural Heritage (SNH) and the Royal Society for the Protection of Birds (RSPB). Since the project began in 1975 many local folk have also helped this spectacular bird return to its former haunts.

1

Sea eagle names

The sea eagle has many names in many languages, not least in English.

Perhaps the oldest used in Scotland is 'Erne' from the Old Norse, which still appears in many placenames, especially in Orkney and Shetland. And it is a useful one to know for crosswords or Scrabble!

'Sea eagle' has been in use for a long time now, and it is only recently that the ornithological world has tried to standardise bird names in English by adopting 'white-tailed eagle'. This may result in the loss of many beautiful local names of birds, like 'peewit' for 'northern lapwing', 'whaup' for 'Eurasian curlew', or 'hedge sparrow' and 'dunnock' for 'hedge accentor'. Some would prefer our largest bird of prey to have the equally large, fuller title 'white-tailed sea eagle'. Confusingly, young sea eagles do not have a white tail at first, while young golden eagles do have a conspicuous white tail.

The general public are well used to 'sea eagle', and many researchers and members of the project team, still use the handy term 'sea eagle' that was used in early bird books, and in the first reintroduction attempts. It is also a direct translation from many of the names used in other countries throughout the bird's range.

What's in a name?

The sea eagle has long enjoyed a near mythical status in the Gaelic speaking areas of Scotland.

GAELIC	ENGLISH
Iolaire chladaich	shore eagle
Iolaire mhara	sea eagle
Iolaire ghlas	grey eagle
Iolaire sùil na grèine	eagle with the sunlit eye
Iolaire bhàn	pale eagle
Iolaire fhionn	white eagle
Iolaire bhreac	speckled eagle

What are sea eagles?

The sea eagle is the fourth largest eagle in the world and is Scotland's largest bird of prey. Its wingspan – an impressive two and a half metres – is bigger than that of the golden eagle, usually considered the king of birds.

With a longer neck, short wedge-shaped tail, broad wings and clumsy looking flight, the sea eagle is more reminiscent of a vulture. Where the golden eagle tilts its wings upwards when soaring, the sea eagle holds out them flat. Both species have yellow legs, but those of the golden eagle are feathered down to the foot, while the sea eagle's are bare.

In Gaelic the sea eagle was sometimes *Iolaire ghlas* (grey eagle) and indeed the adult can often look quite grey. The head and neck can be especially pale, rather reminiscent of the American bald eagle, a very close relative. Occasional white birds have been recorded – *Iolaire bhan* (pale eagle) – and indeed the very last widowed bird, still maintaining a lonely vigil on its nest in Shetland in 1916, was said to have been an albino. The islanders knew it to be about 30 years old when it finally disappeared two years later.

The sea eagle only gains its famous white tail as an adult, when about five years of age. When it first fledges the juvenile is a chocolate brown colour, with a dark grey beak and dark brown eye. Over several annual moults it gradually attains adult appearance – the sunlit eye, yellow beak and light-coloured plumage.

White-tailed sea eagle talons (left) and golden eagle talons (right).

Golden eagle adult

Golden eagle juvenile

Buzzard adult

Sea eagle adult

Sea eagle juvenile

Golden eagle

- legs feathered down to the foot
- length 75 to 85 cm
- wingspan 2 to 2.2 m
- weight 3 to 6.5 kg
- habitat: high peaks and upland areas, very occasionally coastal areas
- will catch and eat grouse, ptarmigan, hares and rabbits. Also eats dead sheep and deer
- short neck, long tail
- normally silent

Sea eagle

- bare legs
- length 70 to 93 cm
- wingspan 2 to 2.45 m
- weight 3 to 7 kg
- habitat: rocky coasts, offshore islands.
- will catch and eat live fish, seabirds, rabbits and also carrion
- long neck, short tail
- can be quite noisy, yelping or croaking calls

4

Many sea eagles released in Rum bear coloured leg rings (as do some fledged abroad), so if you are lucky enough to be close enough to read the colour combination, please report it to SNH or RSPB

Nesting   Neadachadh

As its name suggests, the sea eagle is normally a bird of the coast. The golden eagle, which has enjoyed some respite from persecution in the past, is found in more remote, mountain retreats. But sea eagles can also be found around lakes and rivers further inland, and sometimes in open farmland.

In Scotland sea eagles nest safely at the top of tall trees, constructing bulky nests of large sticks and branches. Where tall trees are in short supply, such as in parts of northern Norway or the west of Scotland, the bird is content to use broad cliff ledges, needing little in the way of a nest structure but often with a small tree in front. Sometimes, on small, undisturbed islets offshore, the nest is even placed on the ground. Being more tolerant of neighbours than golden eagles, sea eagles can nest quite close to one another.

An eyrie in a treetop can be quite a bulky structure

Sea eagles often rear twins

Breeding Briodachadh

Courtship often begins over the winter, but intensifies in early spring. The pair will sit near the nest together or fly around for long periods wing-tip to wing-tip. Occasionally when excitement mounts, one may stoop on another and they even interlock talons, to cart-wheel earthwards with high-pitched yelping.

But more often than not, such behaviour involves young birds reacting to an attack from an adult, or even trying to snatch food from them. The pair will defend their territory from intruders, young or old, but usually seem more tolerant of golden eagles than the goldens are of them.

Two, sometimes three, eggs are laid from mid-March into April and are incubated, by both sexes, for 38 to 40 days. It is not uncommon for two, and even three, young to survive together amicably in the nest. This is in contrast to the golden eagle where - especially if food is in short supply - the bigger chick from the first-hatched egg will prevent the younger bird from getting enough food, and perhaps even attack and kill it.

Cartwheel display used in courtship, but also if fighting or when young attempt to snatch fish from adults

Juvenile sea eagle partly covered in down

Feeding   Beathachadh

Both species of British eagles can have a very varied diet. The golden does best where rabbits, hares, grouse and other medium-sized prey abound, while the sea eagle can easily supplement its diet with seabirds and fish.

In Shetland of old, it was believed that the sea eagle could charm fish to the surface, where they rolled around on their bellies, offering themselves up to the predator hovering above. Some superstitious fishermen even smeared their baits with eagle fat to improve their catch. It is true that sea eagles are quick to exploit spent salmon after a spawning run, or disabled fish that have been swept up to the surface by whirlpools and strong tidal currents.

Although it shares with ospreys spiky soles on its feet, the sea eagle does not plunge dive. Instead it will snatch fish from the surface with barely a splash. It is not averse to stealing prey from otters and gulls, and will even follow fishing boats to take discarded fish.

Both golden and sea eagles will feed on dead animals, especially while they are young and inexperienced, or over the winter when live prey may be in short supply. Thus, in bad springs or in areas with heavy mortality in sheep, both adults and lambs may be scavenged. Indeed, it was for this very reason that birds of prey, and sea eagles in particular, were persecuted so strongly in the past. With their confiding and sociable habits, and a vulture-like taste for carrion, sea eagles were especially vulnerable to poisoning.

Adult sea eagle with fish, a key part of a varied diet

Adult sea eagle with the distinctive bright yellow
beak and characteristic pale head

Not suprisingly, the carrion in their diet may well include any dead lambs they come across. Occasionally individual sea eagles might be tempted by shortage of other food (or sheer opportunism) to start taking live lambs. To crofters who might have relatively few sheep this can become a problem.

The issue is, however, a tricky one. Research has shown that these birds do not necessarily prove a nuisance every year. Lambs are especially vulnerable if in poor condition due to severe weather or if, for instance, a ewe is unable to defend twin lambs from repeated attack. In some problem areas payments towards assisting sheep husbandry and lamb survival can be justified.

Sea eagle and hooded crows feeding on carrian

Where they live

On a global scale the sea eagle extends across the northern hemisphere from Siberia and Japan to Europe, and south to the Mediterranean and the Middle East. It is replaced by the bald eagle in North America, although it is the sea eagle that has colonised the southwest coast of Greenland.

Despite being so widespread, the status of the species is nowhere certain due to loss of habitat (such as forest clearance and wetland drainage), persecution and pollution. Norway retains a healthy population, recently estimated at around 2000 pairs, and it is from this source that the eaglets have come for the reintroduction in Scotland.

The Isle of Mull is a sea eagle stronghold, along with the Isle of Skye further north

Orkney Islands
Westray · Eday · Sanday
Rousay · Stronsay
Shapinsay
Kirkwall
Hoy · South Ronaldsay

Durness · Thurso · Wick

Shetland Islands
Unst
Yell
Fetlar
Foula · Lerwick
Fair Isle

Outer Hebrides
Lewis
Stornoway
Harris
St Kilda
North Uist
South Uist
Barra

Lochinver
Helmsdale
Ullapool

Portree
Skye
Kyle of Lochalsh
Canna
Rum Mallaig
Eigg
Muck Fort Augustus
Fort William

INVERNESS
ABERDEEN

Coll
Tobermory
Tiree *Staffa* *Mull* Oban
Iona Inveraray

DUNDEE
PERTH
Colonsay *Jura* STIRLING
EDINBURGH
Islay *Gigha* GLASGOW
Arran

NORTHERN IRELAND

ENGLAND

© 2006 Wendy Price Cartographic Services, Scotland, IV1 3XQ.

Sea eagle - 19th century
Sea eagle - present day

0 ——— 30 miles
0 ——— 40 kilometres

N
W · E
S

Sea eagle distribution in the Highlands and Islands. Note the concentration on the western seaboard

From totem to target
Bho thòtam gu targaid

Sea eagles were once a familiar sight throughout Britain. Their bones have been found in a Bronze Age burial tomb at Isbister on South Ronaldsay, Orkney. Perhaps they fed on the human corpses deliberately laid out to have the flesh stripped from the bones by carrion-eating birds. This practice is known from other cultures in the past, such as native North Americans, and even today in parts of India.

A totemic role seems to have survived for a lengthy period into later times, with images of eagles carved into the celebrated symbolic stones of the Picts in northern Scotland. The finest example – and obviously a sea eagle – is from the Knowe of Burrian in Orkney. Sea eagles and ravens feeding on human corpses after a battle are also mentioned in several Anglo-Saxon poems from southern England.

There are records of sea eagles nesting throughout the length of Britain:
- a pair of sea eagles was known to nest on the Isle of Wight in 1780
- another nested on the Isle of Man in 1818 and
- several were known in the Lake District until the 1830s

Old placenames in both English and Gaelic indicate other nest sites throughout Scotland, while in Shetland especially, *Erne's Brae* and *Erne's Hamar* preserve the traditional Old English name based on the Scandinavian word 'Ørn' for eagle. Such placenames, together with records from Victorian naturalists and collectors, reveal that at least 150 pairs of sea eagles once nested in Britain and Ireland. Many others will have gone unrecorded.

This Pictish stone carving from Orkney depicts a sea eagle rather than a golden eagle. Note the massive beak, vulturine form and unfeathered lower legs characteristic of the sea eagle

Mythology Seann-sgeulachdan

We know from the Orkney burial tomb that sea eagles have been held in reverence for at least 4000 years. Their importance locally seems to have persisted into the Iron Age with a superb depiction of a sea eagle on a Pictish symbol stone now in Kirkwall Museum, and in illuminated manuscripts of the Celtic church throughout Medieval Europe. It was held that an eagle could look directly into the sun without harm and it was taken as the symbol of the evangelist St John, who had looked upon 'the sun of glory' to acquire his faith.

It is the golden eagle that is seen as 'the king of birds' and its Gaelic name 'Fior eun' means 'the true bird'. It is not surprising that such a symbol of might and power should be revered by many diverse cultures of the world. An eagle was the messenger of the Greek god Zeus, and of his Roman equivalent, Jove. The legions of Rome marched under an eagle of silver, its wings open ('spread-eagled') and a thunderbolt in its talons. When a Caesar died his body was cremated and an eagle set free amongst the flames - reminiscent of the legendary phoenix, a supernatural bird of the Hittites.

In 800 AD the Emperor Charlemagne united Europe under a double-headed eagle, a symbol known from Babylonian times, which survived to become the national emblem of the Russian and Austrian empires. The bald eagle is the national bird of the United States, while an eagle on a cactus and holding a snake is portrayed on the Mexican national flag. This derives from an ancient myth that celebrates the founding of the great Aztec civilisation.

Such eagle/serpent symbolism is worldwide. In Viking mythology, a mighty eagle sat at the top of an ash tree with a coiled snake on the ground below. A nimble little squirrel had to run up and down the tree conveying insults between bird and reptile! It was said that the flapping of the eagle's wings caused tempests in the world of men. This phenomenon was also attributed to the mighty eagle of Snowdon. 'Mor eryr' is Welsh for eagle and 'Eryri' the name for the mountain. Indeed, in the 12th century it was declared how the golden eagle of Snowdon could predict future events, and in particular foreshadowed war. She would perch on 'the fatal stone' to sharpen her beak before satiating her hunger on the bodies of the slain. This gruesome habit of sea eagles is also celebrated in Anglo-Saxon poetry; the Battle of Brunanburh in 937 AD left behind 'the grey-coated eagle, white-tailed, to have his will of the corpses.'

16

The juvenile sea eagle can be mistaken for a
golden eagle but it has a much larger beak

The Anglo-Saxons also believed that the bones of the sea eagle possessed curative properties, while the Faroese claimed that its yellow claws could cure jaundice. Folk tradition is also rich in stories of eagles snatching human babies, usually rescued unharmed through the heroic efforts of the mother.

Towards extinction
A' dol a-mach a bith

Since habitat destruction and persecution was less severe in Scotland and Ireland, their remote coasts provided the last strongholds for the species into the 19th century. Then, with the spread of sporting estates and better firearms, predators became prime targets and bounties were offered in many places.

Until 1835 in Orkney for instance, up to five shillings was offered for a sea eagle head, while the species figured prominently in the 'vermin' lists of most Highland estates. As sea eagles became rarer, they attracted more attention from egg collectors and museums. That is why by 1900, only a handful of pairs remained – in Shetland, the Shiant Isles, Skye and Rum and Ardnamurchan for instance.

The last known nesting attempt was in Skye in 1916 and two years later the lone, albino female was shot in Shetland – probably the last of these native wild birds in Britain.

Adult sea eagle showing off its short, white tail against a hillside. It has a slow ponderous flight

The return of the native
Fiadh-bheatha dùthchasach a' tilleadh

The golden eagle suffered similarly but it survived in its remote mountain haunts and thus gained respite from persecution during the two World Wars. Although stray sea eagles from the Continent were occasionally sighted in Britain, this species was unable to re-establish. Abroad, it was not faring well either, becoming especially threatened in the 1950s and 1960s from chemical pollutants, such as organochlorine pesticides and industrial PCBs (polychlorinated biphenyls) and heavy metals. These toxins concentrate as they progress up the food chain, leading to breeding failure and even premature death in predators such as the sea eagle, at the top of the chain.

In normal situations any predator is much less common than its prey but, if its distribution and numbers are further limited by human activity, it becomes vulnerable to extinction. It has been illegal in Britain to persecute birds of prey since 1954. But, at that time, Europe's sea eagles were under threat, while Scotland was relatively unpolluted and still offered suitable habitat.

Unlike the osprey, the sea eagle has been unable to re-establish in Britain without considerable human help. It seemed only right that it should be given a helping hand by the humans who had, quite unjustifiably, driven it out in the first place.

Natural hazard - the fulmar

The 1968 sea eagle reintroduction programme threw up a tale that proved that the sea eagle, despite its size, doesn't always have things its own way. The fulmar - a small sea bird - will produce a sticky and smelly oil to defend itself and squirts this on predators. Of the four youngsters released that year three disappeared and one was found covered in fulmar oil - it died days after being found.

Sea eagles in Scotland . . . timeline
Iolaire-mhara ann an Alba . . . clàr-ama

1791 to *The Statistical Account of Scotland* gathers
1799   information on 20 counties and presents
them in weighty volumes. Relying largely on
the evidence of local ministers it notes
developments and trends throughout
Scotland. The sea eagle is mentioned as
breeding in many localities including
Braemar, Inverness-shire, Tongue, Dunnet
Head, and Jura

1793 In Orkney a crown (a substantial amount of
money at the time) is being offered for every
eagle destroyed

1834 *The New Statistical Account of Scotland*
repeats the 18th century exercise noting sea
eagles as present in Dumfries and Galloway,
Argyll and several northern counties

1911 The final breeding success of sea eagles
in Shetland

1916 Last pair nest on Isle of Skye

1918 The last known individual - an albino female
about 30 years old - dies in Shetland

1942 An injured sea eagle is found in
Kincardineshire. Similar sightings noted in
Canna, Inverness-shire (1920) and
Hermaness, Shetland (1949)

1959 First reintroduction attempt in Glen Etive,
Argyll, privately-funded

1968 Second attempt at reintroduction as four birds
are released on Fair Isle. Two disappear
within twelve months, the third shortly
afterwards and the fourth dies in 1969

1975 Third attempt at reintroduction begins on the
Isle of Rum NNR. Despite a faltering start, in
which two of the four birds die early, the
project gains a foothold. Run jointly by the
Nature Conservancy Council (NCC) and the
RSPB, the project gradually succeeds and
over a decade 82 young birds are released

1985 First recorded breeding success of
reintroduced birds

1993 Phase two reintroduction begins with 58
Norwegian birds released at Loch Maree
over five years

2000 The 25th anniversary of the current project
coincides with 25 pairs of sea eagles holding
territory in Scotland. To date they have
fledged 100 chicks in the wild

2003 30 pairs of sea eagles raise 26 youngsters

2005 Up to 2005 there have been 192 sea eagles
fledged in the wild in Scotland

Reintroduction
Cur an aithne a-rithist

In 1959 and 1968 attempts had been made to reintroduce the sea eagle into Scotland. They had, however, failed because only seven birds were released and the efforts had not been continued over a period of time. These eaglets had been brought to Glen Etive, Argyll and to Fair Isle in Shetland but had either died or dispersed.

Unloading the eaglets at Kinloss, each safe in its own cardboard box

In 1975 the Nature Conservancy Council began a full-scale reintroduction programme, to be supported later by the RSPB and other conservation groups. Over the next ten years, up to 1985, a total of 82 chicks (39 males and 43 females) were imported, again from Norway, where the sea eagle population continued to thrive. Since the breeding density was so high and twins were common, only one chick needed to be collected from each Norwegian eyrie, and rarely was the same pair deprived more than once. At six to eight weeks of age the chicks were not quite able to fly.

With the generous assistance of the Norwegian authorities and 120 Nimrod Squadron of the Royal Air Force, speedy transfer was arranged from Bodø (a town in northern Norway on the Arctic Circle) to Kinloss air station and thence to the Isle of Rum. During a statutory, five-week quarantine period, the eaglets were fed on a natural diet of fish, birds and mammals with food dumps being maintained nearby after release. Without parents to show them what to do the young eagles had to quickly adapt to the wild but, as the project progressed, they benefited from the presence of older and more experienced releases still present on the island.

RAF Nimrod crew admire their unusual cargo at Kinloss

A tethered young sea eagle, waiting to be released on Rum
in the mid 1970s

Harald Misund who collected all the sea eaglets
which were sent to Scotland from Norway

Phase one A' chiad ìre

The youngsters survived well and, although most left Rum, they gathered together at other particularly favoured places in the Hebrides. Sea eagles take at least five years to mature, so it was several years until the first breeding pairs established. The first eggs failed to hatch, as did two clutches in 1984. However, in 1985 one of the two pairs fledged - the first wild sea eagle in Britain for over 70 years.

Although no more young eagles were imported, the population continued to grow slowly. Eight pairs of birds, established by 1993, successfully reared 34 youngsters themselves. The RSPB were monitoring the population closely but it was obvious that many of these fledglings came from just two pairs of birds. Thus it was considered necessary to give the population a further boost.

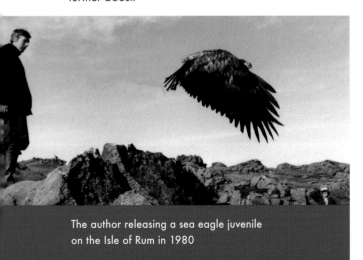

The author releasing a sea eagle juvenile on the Isle of Rum in 1980

Phase two An dàrna ìre

Scottish Natural Heritage started a second phase of releases in 1993, this time based by the shores of Loch Maree in Wester Ross and involving 58 more birds from Norway. By the time this project ended in 1998, there were 18 pairs established in the wild. Some of the Phase two birds were themselves breeding and that year saw nine broods resulting in 13 young birds being raised.

Self-sustaining
Eòin neo-eisimeileach

The next few years saw the number of pairs continue to increase but no more than about a dozen young were surviving each year. Then, suddenly, 2003 proved a bumper year. Thirty-one pairs were established by then and no fewer than 26 young flew from 25 clutches laid. The following year proved almost as successful with 19 young, while 2005 saw 24 young fledged.

Such a significant rise in recruits will no doubt give a great boost to the population, but other possible release sites are being considered. Farmland on the east coast of Scotland could offer further habitat similar to parts of Germany and Poland.

An adult sea eagle carrying a fish

A sea eagle perched in a tree

Protection Dìon

In common with all other birds of prey in Britain, sea eagles and their nest sites are fully protected by the Wildlife and Countryside Act 1981, and the Nature Conservation (Scotland) Act 2004.

It is illegal to:
- shoot, poison or otherwise kill sea eagles;
- disturb them at the nest;
- take eggs or young; or
- destroy nest sites

Heavy fines and even imprisonment may be imposed on anyone who breaks these laws.

Despite this, cases of egg-collecting and persecution still occur. SNH, RSPB and many local people are constantly vigilant. Nest sites are kept under close surveillance by RSPB field staff to ensure that the birds can breed without being disturbed.

The Glengarry Cull
Between 1837 and 1840 it is documented that the Glengarry estate killed 1372 birds of prey, a count that included no fewer than 27 sea eagles. This was by no means an isolated instance.

Even well-meaning members of the public or birdwatchers can disrupt the birds' breeding cycle, keeping the parents off eggs or vulnerable chicks by straying too close and lingering too long. At least four sea eagle clutches have been taken by egg collectors and it is extremely disappointing to see that this illegal habit still persists.

Any animal population will normally have a higher death rate amongst its youngest age group. But being so fond of carrion, sea eagles – especially the inexperienced young– remain particularly threatened by illegally poisoned baits.

Amongst the 25 or so dead sea eagles that had been reported up to the end of 2004, at least six were victims of persecution, mainly by illegal poisoning. Even worse, two-thirds of the poisoned birds were adults. Losing established breeding birds and the long and productive life they may have had, is damaging the efforts to reintroduce the sea eagle.

Island communities co-operate with the police in protecting the nesting sea eagles

Sad Saga in Morar

In spring 2002 a nesting sea eagle was found poisoned in Morar. One year later his mate was also found poisoned. These illegal, barbaric and highly damaging incidents caused outrage locally and beyond. The police and local community are now increasingly vigilant. Both dead birds had been imported from Norway in the mid 1990s. They had been breeding together since 2000.

Where to see sea eagles
A' faicinn iolairean-mhara

A few people remain unconvinced that bringing sea eagles back to Scotland was justified, when so much effort had been put in over the last couple of centuries to get rid of them. But the extermination of the species was little more than a blatant act of vandalism and is something that would not be tolerated today.

Throughout the world, governments are more and more committed to conservation and the biodiversity of life. Indeed when it began, the sea eagle reintroduction in Scotland was seen as a 'ground-breaking' effort which has since paved the way for many other similar conservation projects.

Gradually, if allowed, sea eagles could re-establish themselves in suitable areas all over the country. But, for now, the Hebrides remains your best chance of seeing these magnificent birds. Communities have developed a sense of pride and ownership and consider the sea eagle a valuable tourist attraction. Indeed the presence of sea eagles is now seen as a welcome benefit to a local economy.

Nowhere have you a better chance of seeing sea eagles than in Skye or Mull. During the breeding season, at the Aros Centre near Portree on the Isle of Skye, the public can follow a pair of sea eagles through CCTV cameras set up near their nest. In Mull, the Forestry Commission and local community partnership keeps an observation hide near another nest where the birds and their chicks can be viewed from a safe distance.

28

Birdwatchers scan the sky for sea eagles above Mull

Young and adult fighting over food in winter time. Note the darker plumage and beak of the younger sea eagle

Helping sea eagles
Sibh fhèin agus na h-iolairean

The reintroduction programme is looked after by a UK Project Team who organise efforts to monitor and protect the sea eagles. This is made up of representatives from SNH, the RSPB, the Joint Nature Conservation Committee (JNCC) and the Centre for Ecology and Hydrology (CEH).

As the project continues, it is becoming easier to come across sea eagles in the wild. Most still frequent the west coast of Scotland, but younger birds do tend to wander further afield. One youngster was seen recently in the centre of Glasgow! A few have strayed into England and Ireland but we know of only one bird that has ever made it back to Norway where it is now breeding.

Most of the birds released or bred in Scotland have been marked with metal leg-rings, each with an individual number and return address. You are unlikely to see this in the wild, unless you come across a dead bird. But many of the sea eagles also wear coloured and numbered wing tags, which are more easily visible. Any details of tag colour or pattern are especially helpful in building up a picture of the fortunes of individual birds or age classes.

All sightings help add detail to the success of the project so please send any records, together with your own contact details, to :

RSPB, Etive House, Beechwood Park,
Inverness IV2 3BW.
Telephone: 01463 715000

You can contact the Sea Eagle Project Team through: Species Group, SNH Headquarters, Great Glen House, Leachkin Road, Inverness IV3 8NW

Finding out more about sea eagles Leughadh a bharrachd

Helander B (ed). 2003. *Sea Eagle 2000: Conference Proceedings*. Björkö, Sweden. Swedish Society for Nature Conservation, Stockholm.

Love, J. A. 1983. *The Return of the Sea Eagle*. Cambridge University Press.

Love, J. A. 1988. *The Reintroduction of the white-tailed eagle to Scotland: 1975-87.* Research and Survey in Nature Conservation No 12, NCC.

Love, J. A. 1989. *Eagles*. Whittet Books.

Newton, I. 1979. *Population Ecology of Raptors*. Poyser Books.

Baxter, E. and Rintoul, L. 1953. *The Birds of Scotland (Their History, Distribution and Migration)*. Oliver & Boyd.

Thompson, D. et al (eds), 2004. *Birds of Prey in a Changing Environment.* SNH/BOU/JNCC Conference Proceedings. The Stationery Office.

Cocker, M. and Mabey, R. 2005. *Birds Britannica*. Charles & Windus.

Websites

More details about the project can be found through the SNH website: www.snh.org.uk/publications/on-line/naturallyscottish/seaeagles/ or the RSPB site www.rspb.org.uk/birds/guide/w/whitetailedeagle/index.asp

Also in the Naturally Scottish series...

Scotland has more than 65,000 native species of animals and plants. This series of colourful booklets looks at different aspects of this rich natural heritage from individual species, and even the genetic variations within them, to whole groups within different environments.

Amphibians & Reptiles

Although there are only six amphibians and three reptiles native to Scotland, these delightful animals have been part of our culture for a long time. They feature on Pictish stones and in a play - 'The Puddock and the Princess'.
John Buckley
ISBN 1 85397 401 3 pbk 40pp £4.95

Burnet Moths

Unlike many other species of moth, burnet moths fly by day. They can be easily recognised by their beautiful, glossy black wings with crimson spots. Their striking colouring is a very real warning to predators.
Mark Young
ISBN 1 85397 209 6 pbk 24pp £3.00

Badgers

With its distinctive black and white striped face and short, squat body, the badger is probably one of the most popular mammals in Britain. Packed with stunning photographs, this publication reveals some amazing facts about the shy, secretive badger.
Mairi Cooper & John Ralston
ISBN 1 85397 254 1 pbk 16pp £3.00

Butterflies

There are 30 resident species of butterflies found in Scotland, as well as three regular migrants. The colourful adults may survive for just a few weeks but they certainly brighten up our lives.
Paul Kirkland
ISBN 1 85397 446 8 pbk 40pp £4.95

Corncrakes

Secretive, skulking, rasping, loud, tuneless, scarce . . . all these words have been used to describe the corncrake. But once you could have added plentiful and widespread to the list. Now only a few birds visit Scotland each year. This booklet brings you the latest information on the corncrake and reveals this elusive and noisy bird in its grassy home.
Helen Riley and Rhys Greene
ISBN 1 85397 049 2 pbk 40pp £3.95

Bumblebees

Did you know that Bummiebee, Droner and Foggie-toddler are all Scottish names for the bumblebee? Find out what these names mean and why bumblebees are so special inside this beautifully illustrated booklet. Also discover how you can help the bumblebee by planting appropriate flowers for their continued survival.
Murdo Macdonald
ISBN 1 85397 364 5 pbk 40pp £4.95

Fungi

Fungi belong to one of the most varied, useful and ancient kingdoms in the natural world. Scotland may have almost 2000 larger species with some of the most interesting found in our woodlands and grasslands. This booklet provides an introduction to their life cycles, habitats and conservation. Discover the fascinating forms of earthstars, truffles and waxcaps.

Roy Watling MBE and Stephen Ward
ISBN 1 85397 341 6 pbk 40pp £4.95

Lichens

There are more than 1700 species of lichen occuring throughout the British Isles, and many grow in Scotland where the air is purer. Several different species may be found on a single rock or tree, resulting in lichenologists spending hours in one spot!

Oliver Gilbert
ISBN 1 85397 373 4 pbk 52pp £4.95

Mosses & Liverworts

There are almost 1,000 species of moss and liverwort growing in Scotland, representing more than 60% of the European bryophyte flora. Although they are small plants, they are certainly important ecologically and are also very beautiful.

Gordon Rothero
ISBN 1 85397 446 3 pbk 52pp £4.95

Red Kites

This graceful and distinctive bird was absent from Scotland's skies for more than a century. Now with the help of a successful programme of re-introduction, it's russet plumage and forked tail can once again be seen in Scotland.

David Minns and Doug Gilbert
ISBN 1 85397 210 X pbk 24pp £3.95

Red Squirrels

The red squirrel is one Scotland's most endearing mammals. This booklet provides an insight into their ecology and some of the problems facing red squirrels in Scotland today.

Peter Lurz & Mairi Cooper
ISBN 1 85397 298 4 pbk 20pp £3.00

River Runners

Scotland's clean, cascading rivers contain a fascinating array of species. The atlantic salmon is the best known of our riverine species but others, such as lampreys and freshwater pearl mussels, are frequently overlooked but no less captivating. This booklet aims to illuminate aspects of their intriguing and largely unseen lifecycles, habitats and conservation measures.

Iain Sime
ISBN 1 85397 353 X pbk 44pp £4.95

For our younger readers

SNH's free "all about . . . White-tailed Sea Eagles" leaflet is available from the Publishing Unit at Scottish Natural Heritage.

This leaflet can be downloaded from the Publications area of the SNH web-site or ordered from:

The Publishing Unit,
Battleby, Redgorton,
Perth PH1 3EW
Tel: 01738 458530

SNH Publications Order Form:
Naturally Scottish Series

Title	Price	Quantity
Amphibians & Reptiles	£4.95	
Badgers	£3.00	
Bumblebees	£4.95	
Butterflies	£4.95	
Burnet Moths	£3.00	
Corncrakes	£3.95	
Fungi	£4.95	
Lichens	£4.95	
Mosses & Liverworts	£4.95	
Red Kites	£3.95	
Red Squirrels	£3.00	
River Runners	£4.95	
Sea Eagles	£4.95	

Postage and packing: free of charge in the UK, a standard charge of £2.95 will be applied to all orders from the European Union. Elsewhere a standard charge of £5.50 will be applied for postage.

TOTAL

Please complete in **BLOCK CAPITALS**

Name

Address

Post Code

Method ☐ Mastercard ☐ Visa ☐ Switch ☐ Solo ☐ Cheque

Name of card holder

Card Number ☐☐☐☐ ☐☐☐☐ ☐☐☐☐ ☐☐☐☐

Valid from ☐☐☐   Expiry Date ☐☐☐

Issue no. ☐☐   Security Code ☐☐☐

(last 3 digits on reverse of card)

Send order and cheque made payable to Scottish Natural Heritage to:
Scottish Natural Heritage, Publishing Unit, Battleby,
Redgorton, Perth PH1 3EW Tel: 01738 458530

pubs@snh.gov.uk   www.snh.org.uk